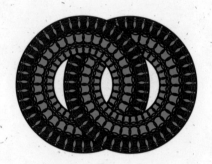

My Painted Warriors

Peggy Penn

My Painted Warriors

CavanKerry ✤ Press LTD.

Permissions, CavanKerry Press,
6 Horizon Rd., Ft. Lee, NJ 07024.

CavanKerry Press Ltd.
Fort Lee, New Jersey
www.cavankerrypress.org

Library of Congress Cataloging-in-Publication Data

Penn, Peggy, 1931-
My painted warriors / Peggy Penn. -- 1st ed.
p. cm.
ISBN-13: 978-1-933880-26-6 (alk. paper)
ISBN-10: 1-933880-26-0 (alk. paper)
I. Title.
PS3566.E475M9 2011
811'.54--dc22
2010049857

Cover and interior design by Gregory Smith
First Edition 2011
Printed in the United States of America

NOTABLE VOICES
CavanKerry ⊕ Press

CavanKerry Press is proud to publish the works
of established poets of merit and distinction.

CavanKerry Press is grateful for the support it receives from the
New Jersey State Council on the Arts.

Contents

Wintering Over   *3*

Deliverance   *5*

Bath   *6*

The Muse Takes a Fall   *7*

The Arrival   *8*

A Summer Day   *10*

Cello Suite   *11*

Cookie the Swan   *12*

Elegy   *14*

First Communion   *16*

Fishman   *17*

Forty Panes   *18*

Gone to Earth   *21*

High and Low   *23*

Hurricane   24

Juliet   27

Leaving Home   28

Love Lies Bleeding   32

Mementos   33

My Brassiere   34

No Poem   35

Orgasms After 60   36

Paradise   38

Refugee   39

Ritual of Dignified Transfer   40

Seeding Perspectives   42

Skunked   43

Smoke   45

Spring Song   47

The Death of William   48

Victory Garden   49

Cemetery   51

Cherry Trees   52

Five Painted Warriors

Ethan ▼ Liam ▼ Matthew ▼ Aidan ▼ Dylan

Everything Comes   57

Ethan Warrior   60

Liam Warrior   61

Matthew Warrior   63

Aidan Warrior   65

Dylan Warrior   67

Acknowledgments   71

Dedications

I have often tried to understand what makes Larry Gelbart so ideal to dedicate this book of poetry to. First of all, I love him. Secondly, he is a wonderful writer, better than I could ever aspire to. Third, he has encouraged me to write from the very beginning of our relationship. It seems, after all, I could go on and on. Outside of marriage, I have always thought of him as my best friend. I could trust him, he made me laugh all the time, he loved my children, and I will miss him for the rest of my life. Is there another definition?

I would also like to dedicate this book to Arthur Penn, whose presence will be obvious to anyone who reads it. It was a grand and wonderful life.

Special thanks to
Molly Peacock, Molly Penn, Owen Lewis, Gloria Loomis
and my publisher,
Joan Cusack Handler, for their unwavering
support of my work.

My Painted Warriors

Wintering Over

Our small hawthorn tree seems to be dying.
The rubbing of its leaves is a dry cough
blent into the rough midwinter air.
Passing the lake lying quiet in ice,
we see the tree become a semaphore
flashing in the sun. My daughter calls,
"We're coming!" Our eyes cry in the cold
as we squint up at the hawthorn's back
where a split is sunk deep in its bark.
We know the culprit; a deer rubbed

the fur of his antlers on her trunk,
flung open her center and gutted
this pale green wound. A spot of dry blood
paints a curl of bark; probably the deer,
too, was young. One magenta root
is exposed from a vole's recent tunneling,
intimidating the other roots—
no one can keep a decent foothold
·standing on one foot. Since we can't restrain
the vole, the deer or the cold, we get

the wire cutters, drag the scoring mesh
across the snow, bring a ladder, stakes,
heavy string, and slowly tie
the origami pieces of the cut cage thing
together. As my daughter sews on
mesh wings to upend it in the spring,
she remembers her arm in a cast,
in her fourth winter: I'd been out pruning
branches when waving her cast, she screamed,
"Don't cut it, don't cut it!"

hot dirt rivers running down her cheeks.
We dragged the branches into the house,
saved them in warm water and promised her
green leaves before the snow was gone.
Every day for weeks she was rapt, studying
the branches—as did I—but with deflating
faith. Finally, two clasped leaf hands appeared
on a branch tip, forcing her knowledge
of regeneration. She clasped her hands
in imitation of the branches and . . . of me.

But the hawthorn doesn't heal; heavy snows
come wimpling the top of the mesh cage;
it looks as though she's taken the veil
in her cold cloister. Three times this winter
I've waked with a pain in my side. Outside
I can hear the deer bump, bumping the house,
scratching a toehold, cracking through the ice,
escaping the lake lying quiet and cold.

Deliverance

for Jill Jakes

Here the river takes us lightly; innocent
of its lower rapid waters we drift
obediently into an unseen world.
Yielding, a pair of herons glides ahead;
concealed by rocks, unspied, they suddenly
sail up, heedless of our pale canoe,
majestically alive and blue! You are
in the stern, piloting us. Riverside,
willow light slides through leaning trees;
flickers dart and hide. Your laughter infects
the air, affects our glide, churns the river till
the whirlpool of circles around my eyes
underlines a gratitude of being there.
I meant to read you a poem, but more
than words, more even than a poem,
your ongoing river restores my certainty,
like an echo finding its wonted voice.

Bath

Lowering
myself into the bath, I know my frame
will widen in the water and like
a skeleton, grateful finally to
close its eyes, I close mine

and the pain stops.

Wishful
in the lap of the bath, I hum
the non-tune my daughter always hummed
when I washed her hair and rubbed it in
a big white towel. She sat as still
as life permits, rearranged the clotted mass
of her hair I carefully disentangled.

Buoyant
in the pond we carried each other
from shore to shore, alternating roles
of mother and child practicing safe
together in our warm, amniotic mirror.

Cold
now, I slip my hands under my thighs
thinking, *we don't deserve the ends we get.*
Grabbing the rubber stopper with my toe,
I watch the sucking begin; our faces
spin into the thin blue lines like those that map
my ankles. The shivers that move up my spine,
seem to spring from the backs of my arms, like fins.
How must it feel, I wonder, to be without
sin, sunning myself on a small rock,
cold and ageless, combing my beloved daughter's hair?

The Muse Takes a Fall

Down to the pond one red maple leaf
falls on a watery shadow bed;
its aureate edges glow like the finish
on burnt roses. Summer's table recalled—
in the heron's grief for the limned crawfish,
sprawled in a mud bowl at the bottom;
it emerges in the sharp light when it knows
the hovering azure shadow is gone.

Sighs of lilac wood phlox, a wide seam of hill
fills with trembling poplars, whose leaves of gold
fold into the brown noises under my foot.
And the smell of the earth revives even
my parents from their loamy, darkening sleep.

Who is leafing through my life, leaving me
to fall from time to time, far flung and deep
as the white ahead falls on bare black limbs
like lines fall on a white page until the end?

The Arrival

It is so windy that summer day
she cannot keep her skirt from blowing
and exposing her long bare legs which end
in new red shoes with heels she keeps turning
round to see. She is thirteen and waiting
alone for her father's train. Her mother
has refused to come, though he is returning
from the war in June 1945.

Heart pounding, she realizes
she's grown three inches since he left,
(five counting the heels). Will he even
recognize her? A secret, she wears
a small brassiere. "Honorable Discharge,"
they said. He is sick, but her grandmother
snorts, "Sick! Sick of what?"

He's sure to feel angry and maybe alone
because his wife stayed home. (But he might
be glad to see me, tell me he's missed me.)
The wind, blowing her hair over one shoulder,
makes her look older. Fleshed out by the gust,
she contemplates time's countless, unjust
seconds, years passed in waiting.

There he stands, frozen on the platform,
staring at her legs; he does not move.
Her cheeks now as red as her shoes, *look down.*
"Only whores don't wear stockings!"
he finally says. Exactly like the bee
stinging her lip but not leaving her face,

his eyes hold her in place as the space
between them turns to stone. Her sliding mind
finds an old Sunday school lesson; Lot's wife,
turned to stone, for one last look at Sodom!

Her grandmother says it is a sin, the war,
her long hair, the shorts she wears in summer,
but her grandmother is wrong. She knows the sin:
she met him at the train with bared legs
while her mother waited clothed at home,
that it was as a woman she has loved
the long waiting time for him. Next day
the pain increases and her grandmother
says, "The flower of blood has come."
She feels a flinty shame—she is a woman;
it has arrived on Armistice Day;
the old war turns cold, and she is to blame.

A Summer Day

New York City, September 2003

The green cathedral, where I sit gulping air
like water, in the body smell of summer,
stretches nets of lace-light through trees to fall
on my lap; one hand rests on the other.
Ring fingers touch and hide a small arthritic
spur. Rowed by women, the rowboats waste no time,
sliding by in a gray Monet blur;
the men lie trailing their hands in the water.
Chaste girls paint their many toenails red,
blue, and green, a feint of dance in pointillist
dots. A wedding party scrambles over
the hill; the Russian bride to bed the Irish
groom with scoured cheeks. In red décolletage,
bridesmaids vine themselves around a blue
gazebo for photos.
An old woman in a wheelchair and
a fur, parrots like a rapper, "Hotdog,
hotdog, . . . I wanna hotdog!"
The groom helps his mother onto a rock, and they
smile in their duet of not forgotten gratitudes.

Cello Suite

1

Legions of bending
barberries—witches' capes—
edge the mountain face.
November sun arrows
the gravesite. I hear them
whisper, *go on, we go on.*

2

Memories like ironies
stick: pine sap.
They never come off
but you smell of life.

3

With you lying over me
over the edge, I slip,
still gripping your grip.
With your hand in mine
I reach for your hand
and we palm each other's
fortune into one more day.

4

Why is there a string
in my chest on which a
cello suite is played?
Every breath a downbow?
I know it keeps the player tired;
I know she will stop soon and rest
from so much music.

Cookie the Swan

for Molly Peacock

It was a small green parrot named Cookie,
hooked upper beak worked like a construction
bucket on a seed: crushing and sorting shell
from seed, hydraulic swallowing: head up,
fast nods backwards (no hands to help), no waaater . . .
satisfied he gently stroked her cheek before
bestowing his twittering kiss—he loved her.
He flew about during the poetry
lesson, happiest on her finger,
the top of her head, under her chin, or
fluttering his wings on her cheek.

If, when speaking, she stroked his wing back
with her cheek, he would prance
on her chair arm up and back, with that
staccato turn of his head; a halo
of gold green enthusiasm!
He rarely ventured onto my head or even chair arm
but accompanied us in the tsk-cluck
of parrot talk, happy as a clam.
When we worked from a single copy of a poem,
our heads bent together over the table,
his screeching cry would bring her out of her chair

and Truffaut-like she changed his day to night
by coaxing him in and covering his cage
till he was in the dark! She was his sun
as much as he was hers. In these small hours
inside the covered cage, perhaps he consoled himself
with images of the lush Courbet painting

of the woman and the great predator bird—
wings outstretched over her resplendent flesh.
Beneath his blinding coat of many colors
glinted talons so strong holding her down.
He would barely have heard the rich winged words
that flew about our minds when she was Leda
and he, the swan.

Elegy

My sister-in-law
    stitched and tucked
my bridal veil with long lacy
    fingers making soft
Swedish noises till I appeared,
    a Vermeer virgin.
She was the only sewer, sister, mother
to wrap me and record my preparation.

She wound me in wedding chiffon
    to be a song for my husband
for the next fifty-five-years.
Now she lies in a shroud of her own
    and time is vanishing.

I see from your hospital window people
    rushing beneath,
days going by, flowing through the streets.
    Long hours stand watch
by your bed in sentinel rows, shifting their weight.
    Hours orbit around our heads
yours in this hour struggles for air under the mask.
    Food hours come and go untouched.
Sometimes a sparkler minute appears, scatters,
    flashes, and falls down dark as your
eyes close again.

You are like cellophane on the bed, transparent
    and soft as the fiberglass you made
into such strong living shapes.

The day is nearly gone; I crawl in beside you,
fold you in my arms. This is the hour of our
        holding; together we will conserve this very
small bit of still dazzling daylight.

First Communion

At twelve I know I have it all mixed up.
Mantras are being said to help me
understand the Easter ritual
of bread and cup of body and blood,
that puts a gardenia on my hat
and orchids on my mother's.
The dry wafer sizzles on my protrud-
ing tongue. Excitement and disgust bring
a rising tide of saliva to my throat.
I try to stay above it so I may
EAT THE BODY OF CHRIST as though he were
a dead animal, hit by a car
that we all leap upon and cut into
slivers. The wafer melts, sweat ripples down,
inking the blue cornflowers on my blouse,
outlining my nipples; trembling, I lean
forward into my hands. "Epiphany," they sing,
passing paper cups of grape juice
which I salt in my mind so it will taste like
blood and redeem me. I am ashamed
of the things I have done and promises
I have made if He will just make certain boys
notice me. Even thinking of my shame
makes my skin crawl with thoughts of them.
I look at my mother: she sits unmoving;
unmoved, as though her whole body were
a cucumber mask. I watch when she peels it
off, hoping for the new face she deserves.
Leaning close I hum, "How big will my breasts be?"
She turns with the face of a falcon whose hood
has just been removed and, with yellow eyes glistening,
says what I know in my heathen heart to be true.

Fishman

A man walks alongside the riverbank
against the flow of the water—eyes
caught by a quivering object. The angle
of the shadow is too steep and inter-
mittently camouflages the fish.

Each solitude, man and fish, accompanies
the other. The fish is careless of the man
but the man is fixed on
that slip of silver hooking in and out
of light. The fish, flashing its shadow play,
is out for food. Each is predatory
in turn: but unequally.

Long ago I took two pennies from
a pink, cut-glass sugar bowl to buy
a beaded licorice gum ball on a yo-yo
rubber string. . . . I saw my father waiting
for me at a distance in anger and knew
this was the beginning of grief.

The fishman paces like a climber who
calculates the mountain; the mountain
does not calculate anything—
it just stands against the sky.

Forty Panes

Rare to see so much red at a funeral.
on this gray day we march into a red church,
red velvet seats, among a maze of blood-red
hawthorn branches, listening to red-hot New Orleans jazz,
we half dance in . . . and oh sure, we partner up.

Trumpets blow! He's dead in the coffin up there,
fled a small town in Utah, wed a wacky,
gifted girl and they became . . . inbred together.
Forty hand-blown panes glisten in ten, tall
New England windows; and eighty cardinals
sing their red songs perched on eighty limbs.
We laugh,

One guy's speech details the contents of Ray's car:
—seven beer cans across the hood like war decorations,
—at least two doors always open,
—an empty catsup bottle,
—half eaten jar of peanut butter,
—matches,
—dog biscuits,
—bait and tackle,
—notebooks whose pens are stuck through the dashboard,
—several pairs of broken sun glasses,
—a cloroxed green tee shirt, three old socks (brown?),
—picture of Sal about twenty—five years ago,
—Chris's wedding picture, recent, lovely.

OH My God, there he is!!—startin' down the aisle,
beer can in hand, naked as a jay bird—
dangle swinging from side to side, yellin',

"I got a list on all you suckers . . . so dontchoo piss on me . . .!"
This is his funeral!! Big yellow shoes still on his feet
but no clothes, and it's a bloody, freezing, October day.

We never saw his feet; too scared to swim;
his father threw him in and nearly drowned him,
so childhood, enchained by paranoia,
passed into fatherhood. I can hear
my daughter speaking. Ray's kid was her best friend.

They played with Edna and Mary, Ray's dog,
named after his two old aunts in Utah.
His wife, Sall, made him a doll to take along,
and I bet it even resembled her, except
for the oversized tin ears, so he could hear
in the next life. (He sure was pretty deaf in this one.)

(Oh My God, He's Back. Now he's outside, frag-
mented through the panes. Multiples of him
are playing a sweet Schubert song. Suddenly
the violin splinters, and a million
memories fall on us like feathers.)

His brother stands up, reads four post war pieces
from Ray's last book . . . suddenly he looks up
and tells us,". . . on Ray's last day, he was so happy
to be able to sit on the toilet and go because
he was afraid he couldn't today. . . .
He knew it was his last time." Suddenly

his brother guffaws, and falls forward
on the lectern, stumbling, choking in tears . . .
people run up. Horns bleat to save him,
"Oh, When the Saints Come Marchin' In" . . . the music
ends in honkytonk jazz; God, its hard not to dance!

Looking for him in the forty panes
we see ourselves, cross-eyed, owlish, broken up.
Imperceptibly the panes have refused
his image, and he is gone. On this nude
October ground, grapes still bend the arbor.
We file across the road to the offered food,
a groaning board. We eat and laugh and talk
and dance, and Goddamnit, some of us cry,
pretending we're not going to die. In this rosy-
gold, nude afternoon, we can see only
dying ahead, and not a hint of spring, none at all.

Gone to Earth

On a day so drear a bird could fall
and its quiet slump would not be heard
in the airless shaft, the morning whistle

calls as the men shuffle up bare hills, feet
moving as though the path were in their blood.
With lamp and bird they go each day to hell

and back to gather pick-ax black diamonds—
coal; the pulley rig lowers them deep into
the narrow shaft, down under the light.

Bedrock. Now flat on flat coal cars, they pump
themselves through unclean air to their digging
stope. From twelve to twelve-ten, another whistle

blows, and they eat a bean sandwich, drink cold
coffee. Four o'clock—the whistle blows: flat on
the flat cars they travel back; hauled up,

they lie coughing on the grass; even the young
ones, trembling rabbits with runny noses,
spit blood, crumbling and black;

incongruous here in the sun, they take a solemn nap.
Eventually their legs collapse, their lungs,
and then the mine. But they leave hidden

pockets behind, empty shafts in the earth.
Seeping walls of brackish water fill the holes,
for whey-faced children (playing on the

sunny surface) to fall down.
No one knows anymore where
they are in the overgrown lacings

of burdock, spurry and hop; a sabotage
of surfaces covering the hidden shaft
until the fallen child cries out.

Eventually the men die and the women,
too, falling to rest in the same earth they dig.
They never die far from the mine.

The hole they fear and know,
always lays underfoot, waiting.

High and Low

for Jane Kenyon

Did you search high and low for the perfect word,
"otherwise"? Are you vulnerable to some,
to others, immunized? No more could I
look inside your word, *"flightbag"* (a small coffin),
and see that small shape, so recently
uncurled, curled back again, falling to one side. . . .
Sometimes I can't find the word, or it won't come,
and neither cadence nor guess delivers it,
only obsession. Some words are too big
to walk inside, others too annoyed to move
over. So we wait, shaky; the word forbidden
to us. Then your dog barks! having found
the smell of spring under snow; the word,
unbidden, plows up through silence and
won't leave you alone . . . (well, one needs the company).

Hurricane

In a field I am the absence of field
Mark Strand

Turning inland, a wild turkey family
in tweed coats scatter together through
high grasses, hunkering down, unable to fly
in this wind.

We are all grounded.
In my pocket there is another hurricane,
another piece of blue note paper,
a letter informing me that my first love,
(a swain from Hunker, Pa.) who loved me
most of his life (we both thought he would always be there),
died ahead of me—which was harder
than losing him the first time.

Marriage was the beginning
of the slow leaving but never letting go
of the thought that the way back was still open
as it had been so many younger times before.

After the sadness I think how kind his wife is
to write and tell me heartbreaking news.
She had written once before,
"He is not doing well," and
I called her. She asked me,
"Can I give him a Percodan tonight
to ease the pain?"
"Oh yes, please give him the Percodan *and tell him
it is from me and forgive him if he still loves me.*"
That is what I want to say, but don't.

"May I talk to him?" "No," she says,
he couldn't hear anymore.
I knew he would have heard me,
but this was her choice.

"If I write to him would you read it to him
really loud?" and she said she would, so I wrote:
I thanked him for his wonderful parents,
the food his mother cooked just for me,
I knew if he heard that, he would remember
our Sundays of love in his bed. We never left all day—
the shade cord knocking against the window sill while
I swam through undersea, lemon-green light . . .
his anemone hand brushes my breast,
we suck air into a world inviolate.

"Does the room feel us move?" I ask him, smiling in the dark.
Clattering, banging words fall to the floor;
this strong need of words endangers the tank—
oh, it will break . . . quiet, yes, quiet . . . we are almost quiet.

A month later this blue note invites me to his funeral.
I do not go.
I would not intrude on their privacy
with his love for me.
I know he would be grateful for me not to come.
It is a gift I wish to give him.

The hurricane is closer now.
No one is left to nail down the boards
of my house, tape the windows, batten down
my hatches. I wait in the basement
with one very dry martini, watching
the yellow, apocalyptic light
roll over the hills.

Now the hurricane is here, but I am staying.
When everything has gone, I will remain,
though I am the place
where nothing remains.

Juliet

The day before spring the earth smells of beetle
birth and wet cantaloupe. A butterfly's
still gauzy face braces on a wisteria
sprig, waking its lilac shake. But the nude
shoots shiver as a freezing rain begins,
first in the morning then again before noon,
until ice turns every branch and twig
into rows of icicle teeth. Juliet,
our passionate spring, upstaged by the old
winter men, is once again bereft
of her true warm love and falls into sleep. Howling
winds make the ice teeth glitter and click, white
with rage, against the lengthening of the light.

Leaving Home

for my boys,
Ethan and Liam

"Its ways were ways of pleasantness and all its paths were peace."
PROVERBS 3:17

Death

The night before, a flying squirrel
left a rabid trail even the dog
wouldn't sniff. In my effort not to slam it,
I left the door open . . . my grandmother said,
"*You* brought the succubus into the house."

Waves break running from his eye.
He is drowning, my beloved grandfather . . . .
His great lungs fill with water;
I can hear him sloshing in his earth bowl.
With every breath, I say: Love me best.

The fingers on his large hand always working
in unison, shoveling, scooping up
an orange, or buttoning his constant vest.
Always melancholy, I lean against
his chest and let him stand against my sadness.

He reads me the funnies; my finger follows
every line. "*We are true blue,*" I say,
"blue like the deep grotto I once saw
in West Virginia." He smells of Prince Albert
pipe tobacco; I know it is named for him.

He lost his candy store in the Depression.
Now he runs a suit club, where for a dollar
a week, someone wins a free suit and vest.
He makes twenty-five cents on every dollar.
Jingling the quarters in his pockets,
he feels like a failure, except with me.

Runaways to the carnival, we throw balls
at hairy dolls, darts at heart-shaped balloons,
dare each other in bumper cars. Our nine-year
old weapons: shrieks and howls, darts and balls;
till, swooney with excitement, we escape her,
rejoicing. He is my real beginning.

She sends him panting up the long hill, back
to the store for the constant exchange. Watching
him always in the wrong, and amenable to her,
I scream, threaten murder, madness, and sob
till his red-faced return; he hides a secret

licorice gum ball for me. In the cellar
beside the furnace, he brushes my hair,
I suck the candy. When my father
punishes me, he waits where I can see him.
He was my father's constant guest, I tell
myself well into my fortieth year.

The Worst Story

My grandmother locked his mother in their attic
and literally starved her. My terrified
eight-year-old mother slipped her snippets of food.
The worst story is: *where was he, my savior,*
not standing up to my four-foot-nine-inch

grandmother, master of the short rib punch?
His face shone down on me but with no con-
secration of power. Unbelievable.
My denial. I skipped my analysis
twice protecting my Ozymandias.
Implicated, compromised and footless
in this world, I was his willing accomplice.

For his funeral I am allowed to wear
my mother's orange corduroy dress, puff
pockets over the bosoms. I am dressed
older than nine but after all . . . he loved me
best. I sit with him laid out in the coffin,
warming his cold hands, promising if

he'll open his eyes, just for me, I won't
tell *anyone*! My mother doesn't cry
for her father, even when the attractive
minister smiles at her. Is she angry
her father didn't rescue her from her mother?
Is she jealous of his "out-of-town woman" . . . or of me?

Recurrent Dream

He slides his hand under his hat
slowly moving it up to sit on his
planetary head. As though moving in oil,
he folds his overcoat carefully
over his arm; he is ready. His mouth opens
in an O but no sound comes out. . . . "*WHAT?* . . . "

I say, "*Wait for me! Don't put on your hat!*"
Turning toward the home-before-me
in his seven-league boots, he strides across
an empty landscape until I am a speck.
The day . . . continues to shine brilliantly,
like freshly minted tin; you would think death
couldn't make a dent.

Love Lies Bleeding

I cut my Love Lies Bleeding from the garden.
Like a rosary dangling from my pocket,
it coils from vase to table.

Its dark red balls are like the rosary
of revenge my grandmother carried, a bit
like the fringe trimming the chaise where she lay

for one whole year, her jilted cries accusing us
of stealing, tufts of her hair scattered on the floor,
her mouth foul with shouts. We closed the windows.

The plant is wilting. . . . This is, I suspect,
my last cutting, for it seems unenthus-
iastic, and resembles, in its redness,

a suicide in progress. She could have left
that room, exiting through the window, climbed
over the roof, and down my cherry tree.

By chasing me flying through magnificent
landscapes, consoling herself, she could have
written a poem for me to hear eighty

years later, and I would have had a different
mother. But she stayed, and every day on
every bead, she prayed, *Please God, let him die.*

Mementos

Can you hear that?
The dead are breathing!
You can feel it against your wrist hairs
if you lean in close.
Their eyes are shut tightly against the light,
lashes, slightly wet.

Why do you have them curl their skin
into dry wood shavings
that only fall to their sides?
Why puff out their cheeks like
the plump cheeks of trumpet players,
ballooning out songs? They are silent

like folded things at the back of a drawer,
mere mementos of themselves.
Is that your plan? Have you made up your mind?
I can take them out and look at them
though I know—love is forbidden.
But when I lean forward carefully to

pick them up, they begin a quiet dusty crumple.
I know it is you who does that!
Are you saying they are *more* dead than alive?
Is the decision already made?
Please don't shut the door; there is one
I am still particularly fond of. . . .

My Brassiere

My first nude satin brassiere strap
repeatedly, insistently, slips down
my arm; its satin caress whispers,
"Careful, you're slipping." Has one small
bosom suddenly grown smaller, refused
to fill its cup, hold up its side? What if
her twin falls, exposing the highly
configured nipples to the world, jouncing
faces for every subway rider to see?
They say our cover-up is responsible
for the loss of our sense of smell? What
is coming toward me as we tear through
this tunnel? Kisses or Cleopatra's asp?

My longing for a brassiere is as strong
as my mother's shrieking laughter; *"You're so small!"*
It's the only thing that keeps me from running away—
erasing in a smear of lace my
out-of-home arousal points, battening down
in satin my surcingle sex. To stay, I need
something as strong as the look that boy
put somewhere, burning inside me last night
at the high school dance.

No Poem

I can't write poems anymore; each time
a line springs up a bar goes down, and a red
light *flashes*, "DO NOT ENTER!" But why,
I ask, am I being kept out of my mind?
Soon I will sink from these coiled lines stuffed
in my pockets and ears that can't appear
without paper, white as clematis, and ink.
"STOP DIGGING! THERE IS NO TRUTH HERE!" The man
riding the mulcher proudly sprays his work behind
him as he cuts through air and grass, hoping
to meet the girl with the forsythia hair
blowing behind her; he won't . . . in spite of
the big hard-on he'll have for her tonight. "NO!"
screams the bar, testy at their mere mention,
"THEY MAY NOT MEET!" Question: If I dream
of them hiding by night amidst evergreens,
lured by the call of a blue loon, can
they have sex without speaking a word?

Orgasms After 60

Old love is solid
smooth as a pane of glass
all wrinkles disappear . . .
then just when I think
you don't need me anymore
you do
and we stroll this hill of bed
                in lilac air . . .

Afternoon acrobats—
even in pillow sacks, we find
new angles of entrance,
you promise
to protect my elbow,
I, your knee, and of course,
our joint metatarsals . . .

Resting . . .
grateful for the lull
between comings—your
fingers hum on my spine
I hang from the hair
at the back of your neck—
it is you who keeps me from falling
when the waterfall pours down my
arms . . .

Now we stretch
murmuring peace . . .
we groom a bit

you show me
your leg rash,
almost gone
so faint . . .
as we fold into the fleece of sleep.
I wake looking into your face
you are my sorrow and my ladder up,
lying here you put on my seven-
league boots and say, "Go, Puss!"
I set out and conquer us . . .

That day we had three . . .
and I was too embarrassed
to ask for a fourth.

Paradise

Dinner past, I take an orange upstairs.
I rub my various limbs with oil, softening.
Staring for hours at my tiny, china
figurine. She is perfect: yellow hoop-
skirt, petticoats gleaming in the streetlights
through my window. Sitting at dinner
my father threw the cut-glass salt shakers
at the tinted mirror behind my mother's
head; they held only a few grains of rice.
Screaming, as though from a very small space
I can hear her words: imperfection's price is
emptiness. I hold the orange's cool pockmarked
skin against my face, ad-libbing paradise.
How to be a girl is written on the faded,
flowered wallpaper around my crib.

Refugee

From a haunted dream she flies, my fugitive
bird, wrapped in her blanket; she presses
at the seam between my door and the floor
where my grandmother stuffed rags to keep out
wind, drifting snow and strangers. My small child

nudges my automatic body from
its dreaming bed; I cannot resist her . . . instead,
I wrap her up in a tiny chrysalis
and stroll to her bed, folded together,
sharing the air in gulps of half-lit stories

and song: hers and mine. Now she comes and goes
on her own. I beg
and suffer and scheme for bits of time,
I catch any bone she throws and hold it,
under the memory of spring's return . . .
when Persephone, my shining peony,
safe from theft and cold, with me entwining
the irony of who keeps whom safe.

Ritual of Dignified Transfer

I should say dignified transfer   Monday night

      two coffins are transferred
            the week begins

suddenly I hear a yelp of pain   mine?
        a family member cries out—
two guys   friends Jack and Perry   both killed
            friends from California

the plan is to give families
        a fifteen-minute glimpse of the proceedings of
           transfer—*that's all*
        but families are kept three hundred feet away from
          the plane
no closer
      a new Pentagon policy
families can't touch the coffin but medical technicians autopsy
and prepare the bodies   for the funeral

      the families turn toward home
"flashing" red and blue lights as escort
           to the mortuary
prepared bodies are placed in a bag
      ice packed around them
         for the final trip

        home.
           home on a small twin chartered plane

the first arrival of cases/coffins comes
after the media ban was lifted
brought thirty-five journalists
now the number has fallen to a count we can't see through the
    mists
            but now the number has fallen
to sometimes a single photographer
for the ap

families must ask permission to talk with the news media
                  only once
David Pautsch, 55, from Iowa said
"I'm proud that Jason lived and died for a purpose.
I want people to know that."

when the boy's body arrived at the funeral home
David wanted to see his son's body.
"I wanted to know it was him.
I couldn't identify my son from the waist up
    but when I see his feet, I *know* his feet, I know the *hair*
    on his feet."

    another woman's cry
        too close to me
the funeral ritual was distant
and minimalist,
        Mr. Pautsch said it was fit for a president
            the procession stretched 3.3 miles

Seeding Perspectives

A cardinal sings
his red song in the forest
re-creates my heart.

Basho, are you there?

" . . . twin butterflies
until, twice white
they meet, they mate"

I sit in the garden's
lap. Crooning wind
releases leaves;
they keep time . . .
unafraid of mov-
ing or being moved.

When I gather
dry hulls to burn
I wonder—are they
afraid? Some of you,
I explain, will last
longer, but all of you
have seeded yourselves
to lie *alive* be-
neath the ground.
Oh envy.

Skunked

Skunked on Vicodan I go to Armani's
final sale, lured by a corps of suits,
pinafores of surety. Hanging flawless
and empty, they resemble a pre-op
hospital room waiting for bodies
more than a rack at Bloomingdale's. My God, I hear
muttering sounds, resonating from
armpits, open bottoms, empty
sleeves . . . judgments, criticisms, true Kafka!
Why is no one else here—only a young
 blond man, folded into a corner?
"Where are the bodies?" I quip.
Out having their knees lifted or
their faces replaced?" No answer.

I hold a suit against me, still the stir
of disapproving voices, obediently
put it back on the rack. "LISTEN," I whisper,
"I need this suit to *like* me, make me
acceptable, fix me up, *not let me die.*
if my cells scatter under the knife,
it must protect me from reassembling
as somebody else! I can't wake up,
look in the mirror and say, 'Nope, that's not me!'
I need hope, I need to be a more *suitable* me!"

Home, I hang up two slithery black
Armani bags that hold the suits, one for each
worshipful, surgical occasion—two hips
impeccable, absolute black, and
a tweed for my knees.

The phone rings—a friend calls
to tell me my plastic surgeon has tried
to kill himself . . . ! I take another sliver
of Vicodan. One for my left knee.
Covered with a fine dust from my pill splitter,
I can always lick my hands if I feel too much pain.
My friend says his wife cut him to the quick
with an affair. Terrified to picture
him leaning over my face, knife
in hand, while his tears splash into
my cuts *as he turns the knife on himself.* No.

I find myself *running* to the phone
and in my best bended-knee voice, I tell
the knee surgeon how much I *welcome*
the knife, the buzz saw, the garden shears
the heavy twine and the twenty-two staples,
and what's he doing tomorrow? I hang up and
limp to the nearest red wine I can find.

Smoke

My God, nearly all writers smoke!
That summer sitting on the porch listening to him
I watch him draw in the last two puffs
till he is tearing and squinting but the second
squint is an assembly of me—me
as he would make me. Laughing and coughing he leans
forward to stove the butt, breaking my gaze—
to think outside it—his finger tips rubbing together,
Are you reaching for a precise word to describe me?
"Is there a goddamn pen around here?"
Carefully, he pushes his ashes into little pyres.
He hooks his thumb in his belt while
I pour, sweeten, spoon, and stir his tea.
he's watching me—the word assembly taking shape.
your poetic incarnation allows his face to rest.

He is lounging in my voice. "Beautiful" he says,
"is there more?" What, tea or me? My heart rate is up
the-I'm-about-to-jump-up-for-more-tea behavior is taking
      place
when the writer says, "Look, wait! Stay . . . say a bit more
about yourself."
His eyes move across me to the margin.
He reaches into the empty package, ah, one more!
If he'd had none would he have cut me off before the
lover came on the scene? Four feigned taps on the back of his
      hand
as pieces of me are separated and recombined.
He says, "Because your mother . . ." *No!* but
that's another story, isn't it? I try to hold on but it's too late—
I have a crush on him. Satisfied

he rattles, "Fascinating! you're just . . . "
he holds up the match. *Wait—I'll do it!*
I breathe, *it will give me pleasure!*
Smiling he looks only at his cigarette for a long time
as I strike his match; it flares hot on a hot summer day;
we inhale the smell of sulphur and he watches me
as though reading his proof: his eyes pause,
looking up, to the right, then back at me, still smiling . . .
woman's body white as paper . . . and . . . you can feel it,
you are becoming literary.

Spring Song

On winter ground
still the color of sheep,
a layer of thin
mirrored glass
covers small pools of water.

Every tip, point, segment and clove
chip away at the tightly sewn earth,
which finally cracks a smile,
and lets them through.

First crocus blades,
the small knives
that saw through winter's transparencies,
know when it's time
to cut up toward the sun.

Curved crescents of willows yellow the world.

Spring's ploy:
to dangle joy
till daffodils spill
and miniature greens
on the tree's ends
make a haze of nets
that stretch as though
spring dwells green
behind a screen.

From here I see a child of three
singing to a robin,
jingle bells.

The Death of William

He was my Shakespeare; he gave me endless joy.
The nurse came in to change his bed
and dry him off a bit—
he grabbed her arm and bit her.
She screamed as blood ran down her arm;
I knew he didn't mean to harm.
I stood between them and asked,
"Would you like a kiss?"
"Oh yes," he said, his eyes aglow
and then he wept with bliss.
Her wrist still pouring blood,
as he raised his mouth to mine.
"I love your poetry, your figure, even your
      fright;
your love power over me remains
throughout the day and night."
He beat the bed and tried to speak
but couldn't make a word.
"Goodbye, my love," I whispered.
Whereupon he died.

Victory Garden

"In the fall when I'm gone, rake the garden
into a big pile and burn it down.
. . . Take care of your mother;
she's like a moth
fastened to the screen—wanting in. . . .
She doesn't realize she's already there."

The victory garden, my basic training
in being left, gives me a way to suffer with
you, wear myself out marching its edges,
jump the hurdles of eight-foot sunflowers,
mow 'em down with my big knife.
I wear your clothes, pants rolled up,
several layers of old khaki jackets.
I fall on my trimming knife—a small cut
barely felt under the sweaters.

Rations I eat under the arbor
which gives me great grape camouflage.
I put up a picture of Betty Grable on my
wall just under the picture of Jesus Christ.
My worry:
I never tell you that when you take me
on your visits to the insane asylum
and ask me to dance with the insane
patients—*they frighten the wits out of me.*

We can share secrets now
because who knows about tomorrow—then
the day comes to set fire to the garden.
I rake for two weeks, aim my flamethrower,

throw my pile of matches to the large dry center
(packed down like you said),
ready with water buckets by my side
for any emergency. . . .
An enormous roar goes up.

Cemetery

We pass a cemetery
the size of a small house
smack up against the road,
leaning its elbows,
resting on a low stone wall;
tombstones askew
standing in rows,
holding each other up
like bad teeth
stained green, lean,
the stony names rubbed out.

Somebody wants to buy it!
"Great location for a deli
or a self-pump gas station,"
says the sign.
What will they do with the bodies?

Disembodied from their
"final resting place,"
homeless, restlessly dragging
their grassy manes. . . .

Cherry Trees

The usual punishment for me was
to be sent to my room. But nobody
realized I could climb out over the limb
of a huge cherry tree, escape down
the cherry tree down into the backyard
and away. At some point they would find me
either for dinner or lunch or I would miss
a meal whenever they thought the punishment
was appropriate. I would sniffle a little,
rub my eyes and behave in a manner
that looked like I had received a proper
punishment. In fact, that wasn't the case.
About age ten I figured out
that I loved to eat cherries, mostly the
cherries that grew on my cherry trees.
They were four trees and huge. No one knew I had
escaped my punishment and had a wonderful
time all by myself. I realized I was a
wonderful climber and could make it all
the way down the cherry tree, any of them.

I suddenly thought since I ate so many
of the cherries, it would be very smart
of me to pick the cherries and sell them
for ten cents a box. But where would I get the box?
I had to get those little wooden boxes
that they sold cherries or blueberries or
strawberries in and I could charge ten cents
a box and by the time our vacation
 to the lake was ready I would have made
at least fifteen dollars. I would save the fifteen

dollars until we went to Lake Erie
in the summer and I would use it on
the rides in the amusement park which was
adjacent to the cottages on the
edge of the lake. It was one of the few
things I could do on my own.

Five Painted Warriors

Ethan ▼ *Liam* ▼ *Matthew* ▼ *Aidan* ▼ *Dylan*

Everything Comes

When we first dig the pond
I want to plant sedge;
you say, wait, the birds
will bring it on their feet.
I cheat and plant "Meadow in a Can,"
because I can't wait.

*

November:
neighbors are laughing, we have made
this *crater*! Is this your *battleground?*
they ask—abort the whole pond thing!
I wear a path around its winter edge,
howling into the big mud mouth,
protesting emptiness.

*

You are the believer it will fill
as surely as you sit in the church pew
thigh to thigh with me. In winter
we argue by phone; you are leaving me
with a big raw hole in the ground,
its bald roots, scarified: wonky
nerve ends unable to find comfort
under the snow: too cold, too sad to grow.

*

Spring:
the dogwood's white cups
pink up, shivering in excitement,
so *neon green* is your return.
Together we pull out and burn
the duckweed slowly choking

the throat of our muddy puddle—
surely! it is *water* trickling in!
Climbing red columbine intertwines
with sedge, bonfires lighting
the pond with small red flames.

*

Three more springs:
the second baby sleeps
from room to room. We fret
about a distant friend
who hasn't called.
We practice sleeping
in the afternoon;
young Mozart's music
travels through the air.
Time is plain. . . .
Each drop of day hangs
Heavily . . . lambs bleat for grain;
It's only four o'clock again. . . .

*

Even in a pond an undertow exists:
one day a line plays
through your familiar face
and stays: age, making us new.
Winters come with elegies:
Sister, father, two mothers,
then, our oldest friend. . . .
Bare branches shake
in the breaking storms—crack off.
A bloody red euonymus,
growing on the edge of the pond,
doesn't, damn it, die.

*

Thirty years:
two truckloads of white sand
make their summer beach—
the size of a postage stamp.
Down the hill rolls the troupe
of little painted warriors, hoops of
light falling in feather towel-capes,
ready to do their rain dance.
In the rain, long legs land. Nothing less
than enchantment, I chant and disappear.

*

Floating beyond the middle
of the pond, already feeling
the coolness of night,
water up to my ears
eyes on the sky,
I wait for your dive
knowing it will come,
everything comes.

Ethan Warrior

The world was frozen-gray-icy. . . .
Everybody waiting for some sign of spring,
no matter how small.
A pot boiled with a cut of meat
surrounded by root vegetables.
Ethan's very small face peered through a hole
In the frosty window he had rubbed with
His small fist. He couldn't quite see who was
Making their way up the walk to his front door.
The snow was starting again—recognition!
He began to jump up and down
When he saw us.
The door opened and we blew in.
"*Nonny!*" he shouted,
"Where have you been this long, long day!"
He took both our hands and drew us in.
We were back after many storms,
Loving him as much as we usually do,
And we were three happy people facing
An afternoon together of warm joys.

Liam Warrior

My third grandchild, Liam, is quiet and often fixed in concentration as though he were a still entity in the garden, a sculpture or a small tree. Although he hugs you generously outside of a game played together, it's rare that he hangs around waiting for your contact. With his brother and cousins he is cheery, participatory, not mysterious and still just as beautiful. My first memory of Liam in Italy was taking a giant run and leaping into the pool reciting Emily Dickinson's "I'm nobody, who are you, are you nobody, too?" Splash! The jingle in it clearly appealed to him; and still looking a bit like a naked baby with sloe eyes, he chirped out merrily a rhyme that had caught him. Since in Italy people eat pasta with every meal, he did too. Nobody ever had to ask him to eat dinner; he always did. He was happy there, and a quiet, small attachment grew between us. If he felt bruised, like a flower that had been in your hand too long, he would become quiet, his large eyes floating in tears, and usually go to where his mother was and talk it out. I remember writing in a book I once gave him, "Liam is a mystery, you can't wait to turn the pages." In truth I seem to remember the phrase as one I got from Arthur, or Boppy, as Liam called him, and I wrote it in a book I gave him.

The course of our day in Florence was that we always made a trip somewhere, even just into town which was only a twenty-minute drive. We saw so many points of interest that were in Florence, perhaps the best being the Leonardo da Vinci Museum. The kids have never forgotten that museum and still remark on it to each other and to us. The usual shape a big family vacation takes is for everyone to get along most of the time; but on odd occasions, there are small rivers with no bridges to cross them. A moment like that happened between me and one of the other adults. It was painful to experience (it did not involve Liam) and was very hard to get over. I think both of us suffered because an unkindness had been done, (according to me) whereas the other party thought I was being too dramatic. Possibly.

On one of these days my daughter Molly and I decided to go into Florence, just the two of us. We were going to go shoe shopping. Driving in the car from Cantina to Florence, Molly said to me, "Mom, Liam said to me this morning he noticed that you were very sad, he could see it in your face, and would I, while we were looking for shoes, find a little present for you on the Ponte Vecchio from him?" She said, " I told him I would, so now you must choose something as a gift from Liam!" I was very touched. I accepted the gift as people do when they respond to someone who has kindly looked inside them. I suspect Liam had observed that I didn't know how to fix what I had experienced during the past couple of days. His gift was a way of saying: I'm tuned into your face, Nonny; let me try to see if I can change it for you. I chose a pair of earrings that were half blue and half orange, my two favorite colors, and put them on immediately.

I flaunted these earrings, wore them every day I remained in Italy, always comforted by the thought that a nine-year-old boy who watched me more carefully than I gave him credit for had lifted my spirits. Liam, how observing you are in your quietness and what a gentle touch you have. Thank you.

Matthew Warrior

letter to my son, Matthew, on the occasion of his
thirty-fifth birthday

Imagine

Each time I walk through the John Lennon Memorial
I remember you driving alone for thirty-two hours
to bring the old blue Chevy home from Chicago

and hearing on the radio that John Lennon died.
You were grieving through Ohio, Pennsylvania and New
Jersey for the man who wrote the songs of your life.

Near the entrance to the park is a mosaic—
bits of marble that form a sun radiating from its center
in all directions: a mosaic of the word "Imagine."

Today it is raining in the park and
someone has wound a wreath of yellow roses
around the word "Imagine."
Big drops fall as people stop quietly to look.

The word "Imagine" makes me cry.
I feel its power over fallen memory

and all the coming rehearsals; for the
wand is always there in the mind, ready
to make the change.

Imagine, you will be a father;
imagine how everything is wet at first.
Imagine the years of bending toward the small face
which waits to claim you.

All those kisses you will also kiss,
Understanding that between the kisses you are also kissing

Aidan Warrior

to Aidy from Nonny

Oh Best Beloved, His Other Tail Was the Tale of Mother Love

The small monkey was new to the treetops
and, thought of, quite truthfully, as a small wizard
because, Oh Best Beloved, he did not have dark eyes
like all the other small monkeys in the trees but
pale blue eyes and so transparent so you could see the
sea in them with the fish swimming by—they
even reflected the treetops he flew in and jumped from
limb to limb. He made everybody smile because
he was a happy fellow with a fine spirit. When others
heard about his eyes they came from far and wide
to see the wide-eyed blue-eyed monkey who had,
they thought, very special powers and a funky look
because of one more unusual but important feature—
he had two tails, one in the normal
tail spot and one that grew out of the back
of his head. People thought his eyes and
extra tail brought them good luck because
they assumed he had magic and they
were happy just staring into his eyes.
He didn't mind because of his unusual good
spirit and they noticed that he did have special
powers of observation and could see through
things, like leaves. One day swinging limb from limb
he saw a really tiny brand-new baby—a
bird of paradise who had tumbled from its nest
without knowing how to fly. He swooped down
and with his eyes was able to see it hidden

in the leaves, the nest and the poor frantic
mother who was crying on a branch.
He zoomed to her side, the baby in his arms
peeping frantically, and returned it to
its mother. The forest shook with happiness;
everybody peeped and growled and sang
their songs, praising this monkey for his
good deed. Then he swung back to his own mother
and she took him on her lap, winding and
unwinding his extra tail and then we knew,
Oh Best Beloved, his other tail was a tale of mother love.

Dylan Warrior

My wish is to tell you about a particular grandson, Dylan, Matt and Candace's first child, who has a wonderful brother called Aidan and two cousins named Ethan and Liam.

Candace picked me up at the hospital after my first joint replacement (it was my left knee), and Dylan, at age six, rushed up the walkway to greet me and literally tried to carry me down that walkway to the car. He, my cane and I struggled along until the car door opened and I fell safely inside. Dylan kept his hand on my shoulder until I was sitting on my own living room couch. He patted the couch vigorously and said, "Mom, Nonny, I want to have my birthday party here in Nonny's living room!" I thought, "Here?" but said, "Great!" Candace laughed and we began to make plans. I thought, "I'll get a little rest and find a stationary seat the day of the party and it'll work!" It did. I never could figure out if Dylan did that for me, to include me, or if he really wanted the party to be here. I happily accepted either.

Up until last year Dylan's interest in the garden allowed us to often take walks together. Last summer we put in lights so they would go on at night when darkness fell. When we went to Italy and took the whole family, all ten of us, the first morning I got up early and went into the kitchen to find Dylan already there drumming his fingers on the table. "Non," he said, "let's take a walk. I got this place all figured out; I'll show you how it works!" We began our walk. This property was outside of Fiesole and resembled a small farm hidden in the soft hills of Cantina, dedicated to grapes, olives and figs.

We walked a good distance while Dylan explained, "This is where they grow the olives; these are the grape and fig trees." He pointed to a building far away from the main house: "This is where they press the olives when its time". We found ourselves out of view of the house and close to a promontory from which we could see at a small distance, a good-sized swimming pool. "That's where it ends, when you are finished with your day's work!" I had no idea if he was right, but it sounded so attractive. Clearly he was interested in his surroundings. I suggested he talk to the other grandsons and give them the same splendid, thoughtful tour. We passed many happy hours on that little farm, and the four boys under Ethan's direction put on a play every night. The parents were called to enjoy it before dinner. They all swam at the end of the day, having been to Pisa or Lucca earlier. They called out the poem to each other, "I'm nobody, who are you? Are you nobody, too?" followed by a giant splash! They were a chorus of not yet changing voices that sounded all the way down to Cantina. To be perched with our family as we were looking out over the hills and see mighty Florence in its "l'heure bleu" and hear the voices of the grandsons' play behind us, what more could be asked? This summer was indeed the second half of joy.

I want them to love the earth now, the earth I will be buried in, the earth I have not yet seen—the earth that waits on us all.

Dylan, two years ago, looked around his classroom thinking about what was unique about him. He thought, "I bet I am the only one in this class whose grandmother is a poet. Well, I can write poetry too." I was giving a small reading in a community meeting house in Stockbridge that summer and asked Dylan if he wanted me to read one of his poems. He said, "Sure!" Whereupon he wrote a mysterious and beautiful haiku. Seamus Heaney said we must read other poets to sustain the life of poetry we share. Dylan was my other poet. I read his moving haiku, and everyone clapped. Dylan was in the balcony of the meetinghouse with his parents and brother. He stood up to acknowledge the applause by clasping his hands above his head like a prizefighter. He was proud and so was I. Basho, the Japanese haiku master, wrote, "A poet doesn't make a poem, something in him naturally becomes a poem."

At home in Stockbridge, Dylan's interest in the garden abides. We still go on walks that he has already taken while I follow the direction the small, muscular shoulder indicates as it turns in the sun. He looks out from different vantage points and points at what he calls, "This sweet meadow," or discusses the possibility of mowing a field behind it—changing the moving circles of the lower field or planting grasses next to the house: golden (pure gold, no green) grass: Haconeechloa. Indeed, it is great color next to the house and gives a dappled, golden light. The astilbe, tall as a wand, is primarily a shade flower but now comes in such variations and colors that it can live anywhere in the garden. Dylan doesn't know the names of the all the flowers, but I almost do and we have catalogues if we need them. Dylan uses the editorial "we" when he speaks of our plans—hoping I will consent. He sits beside me. I watch those strong young arms holding the chin of his most beautiful head with long white blond hair and blue eyes that sweep the garden and hillsides. We go down to the section of the pond we swim in and come back with yet another idea. We return infected by the green, his favorite color.

I am not a grandmother who takes these four grandsons lightly. Sitting on that rock two years after he died, I thought a great deal about my brother. How much I loved him as a child, how joyful he was, how our eyes mirrored each other. He loved the earth so much as a little boy. I thought of how much he enjoyed digging and what gleeful noises he made at age two. How strongly he held on to my neck! He would love my four grandsons and would walk with us happily. I could tell him how much I still miss him, how much I love him. I reach for his hand.

Acknowledgments

"Orgasms After 60"—*O Magazine*, 2005
"Hurricane"—*MARGIE*, Volume 8, 2009

CavanKerry's Mission

Through publishing and programming, CavanKerry Press connects communities of writers with communities of readers. We publish poetry that reaches from the page to include the reader, by the finest new and established contemporary writers. Our programming brings our books and our poets to people where they live, cultivating new audiences and nourishing established ones.

Other Books in the Notable Voices Series

Impenitent Notes, Baron Wormser

Walking with Ruskin, Robert Cording

Divina Is Divina, Jack Wiler

How the Crimes Happened, Dawn Potter

Descent, John Haines

Southern Comfort, Nin Andrews

Losing Season, Jack Ridl

Without Wings, Laurie Lamon

An Apron Full of Beans, Sam Cornish

The Red Canoe: Love in Its Making, Joan Cusack Handler

Bear, Karen Chase

The Poetry Life: Ten Stories, Baron Wormser

Fun Being Me, Jack Wiler

Common Life, Robert Cording

The Origins of Tragedy & other poems, Kenneth Rosen

Against Consolation, Robert Cording

Apparition Hill, Mary Ruefle

CavanKerry now uses only recycled paper in its book production. Printing this book on 30% PCW and FSC certified paper saved 2 trees, 1 million BTUs of energy, 127 lbs. of CO_2, 67 lbs. of solid waste, and 524 gallons of water.